From Cream to Cheese

The Ultimate Cow's Milk Derivatives Cookbook

While every precaution has been taken in the preparation of this book, the publisher assumes no responsibility for errors or omissions, or for damages resulting from the use of the information contained herein.

FROM CREAM TO CHEESE

First edition. August 23, 2024.

ISBN: 979-8227140241

Written by Jose Maria.

Table of Contents

From Cream to Cheese...1

Chapter 1: The Basics of Milk Derivatives.................................4

Chapter 2: Fresh Creamy Delights 8

Chapter 3: Butter: From Churn to Table 13

Chapter 4: Cheese: Crafting Curd to Perfection..................... 17

Chapter 5: Yogurt: Cultured and Creamy 22

Chapter 6: Indulgent Desserts with Milk Derivatives..................... 27

Chapter 7: Milk Powders and Condensed Milks 32

Chapter 8: Sauces, Dips, and Spreads...................................... 36

Chapter 9: Cow's Milk in Global Cuisine................................. 40

Chapter 10: Vegan Alternatives and Dairy-Free Options............... 45

Chapter 11: Kefir and Other Fermented Beverages...................... 48

Chapter 12: Whey Wonders: Using Every Drop........................... 53

Chapter 13: Ice Cream and Frozen Treats................................ 59

Chapter 14: Condiments and Dressings 66

Chapter 15: Baking with Milk Derivatives 70

Jose Maria

Introduction: The Wonders of Cow's Milk

The Versatility of Cow's Milk

Cow's milk is one of the most versatile ingredients in the culinary world. Its ability to transform into a variety of textures and flavors makes it indispensable in kitchens across the globe. Whether it's a rich and creamy base for sauces, a fluffy foam for a morning latte, or the essential building block for cheeses, butter, and yogurt, cow's milk adapts effortlessly to countless culinary needs.

This incredible versatility stems from the unique composition of milk—its balance of fats, proteins, and sugars. These components can be manipulated through processes like churning, fermenting, and curdling to create a diverse range of products. From the simplicity of fresh cream to the complexity of aged cheeses, milk's potential is limited only by the creativity of the cook.

Nutritional Benefits of Cow's Milk Derivatives

Cow's milk and its derivatives are not only versatile but also packed with essential nutrients. Milk is a rich source of high-quality protein, providing all the essential amino acids needed for growth and repair. It's also a major source of calcium, vital for bone health, along with other important minerals like phosphorus, potassium, and magnesium.

Milk derivatives like cheese and yogurt offer concentrated forms of these nutrients. For example, cheese is a dense source of calcium and protein, while yogurt is renowned for its probiotics, which support gut health. Butter, while higher in fat, offers fat-soluble vitamins such as A, D, E, and K. Even cream and buttermilk, often used in smaller quantities, contribute to a well-rounded diet by adding richness and important fats that support satiety and nutrient absorption.

An Overview of the Most Common Derivatives

Cow's milk can be transformed into a wide array of derivatives, each with its unique properties and culinary uses. Here are some of the most common:

- Cream: Extracted from the top layer of milk, cream is rich and fatty, perfect for whipping, sauces, and desserts. Variants include heavy cream, sour cream, and clotted cream.
- Butter: Made by churning cream, butter is a staple in cooking and baking, adding flavor and texture to a wide range of dishes. Variants include salted, unsalted, and clarified butter (ghee).
- Cheese: Cheese is the product of curdling milk and separating the curds from the whey. It comes in numerous forms, from soft cheeses like mozzarella and ricotta to hard varieties like cheddar and parmesan.
- Yogurt: Yogurt is created by fermenting milk with specific bacterial cultures. It's a versatile ingredient in both sweet and savory dishes, available in plain, flavored, and strained forms like Greek yogurt.
- Milk Powder and Condensed Milk: These shelf-stable derivatives are made by removing most of the water content from milk. Milk powder is often used in baking, while condensed milk, which is sweetened, is key in desserts like fudge and caramel.
- Sauces and Spreads: Milk derivatives are the foundation of many classic sauces, including béchamel and Alfredo, as well as spreads like cream cheese and butter-based compound spreads.
- Ghee: A clarified form of butter, ghee is prized in many cuisines for its high smoke point and nutty flavor.

Each of these derivatives not only serves a specific purpose in the kitchen but also carries its unique nutritional benefits, making cow's milk an incredibly valuable resource in both home and professional kitchens. Whether you're looking to create comfort food classics or explore the art of cheese-making, the possibilities are endless with cow's milk at your disposal.

Chapter 1: The Basics of Milk Derivatives

Understanding the Process: Pasteurization, Homogenization, and Fermentation

The transformation of cow's milk into its many derivatives relies on a few key processes: pasteurization, homogenization, and fermentation. Each plays a crucial role in ensuring the safety, consistency, and quality of the final products.

- Pasteurization: Pasteurization is the process of heating milk to a specific temperature for a set period to kill harmful bacteria and pathogens without significantly affecting the nutritional value or taste. The most common method, known as high-temperature, short-time (HTST) pasteurization, heats milk to 161°F (72°C) for 15 seconds. Pasteurization is essential in extending the shelf life of milk and ensuring that it's safe for consumption and further processing into products like cheese, yogurt, and cream.
- Homogenization: Homogenization is a mechanical process that breaks down the fat molecules in milk, preventing them from separating and floating to the top. This process involves forcing milk through small openings at high pressure, creating a uniform texture and consistent taste. Homogenized milk is preferred for making products like cream, butter, and certain cheeses, as it ensures a smoother, more stable consistency.
- Fermentation: Fermentation is the process of converting carbohydrates (lactose, in the case of milk) into lactic acid using specific bacterial cultures. This process thickens the milk, alters its flavor, and creates products like yogurt, sour cream, and various cheeses. The choice of bacterial cultures and fermentation time can produce a wide range of textures and flavors, from the tangy bite of yogurt to the creamy smoothness

of sour cream.

Essential Tools and Ingredients for Working with Milk Derivatives

Successfully crafting milk derivatives at home requires the right tools and high-quality ingredients. While some recipes are straightforward, others involve more specialized equipment and precise measurements.

Tools:

- Thermometer: A good kitchen thermometer is essential for monitoring temperatures during pasteurization, fermentation, and other processes. It ensures accuracy, which is crucial for the safety and success of dairy processing.
- Cheesecloth or Butter Muslin: These fine-mesh fabrics are used for straining whey from curds in cheese-making and for draining homemade yogurt.
- Cheese Molds and Presses: If you're making semi-hard or hard cheeses, molds and presses help shape the curds and remove excess whey.
- Whisk and Stirring Spoon: These are basic but vital tools for mixing ingredients, especially during the initial stages of cream or yogurt preparation.
- Churner or Stand Mixer: For making butter, a churner or stand mixer with a paddle attachment is useful for whipping cream until the butterfat separates.
- Fermentation Jars and Containers: Airtight jars or containers are essential for fermenting milk into yogurt or sour cream. They keep out contaminants and ensure an even fermentation process.

Ingredients:

- Fresh Cow's Milk: The quality of the milk you start with greatly influences the final product. Whole milk is often preferred for its higher fat content, which adds richness to creams, butter, and cheeses.

- Cream: Depending on the recipe, you may need heavy cream, whipping cream, or double cream. Each has a different fat content, affecting the texture and flavor of the final product.
- Cultures and Rennet: These are specialized ingredients used in fermentation and cheese-making. Cultures introduce beneficial bacteria for products like yogurt, while rennet is used to curdle milk in cheese-making.
- Salt: Salt is essential for flavor and preservation in butter and cheese. Non-iodized salt is typically preferred as it doesn't affect the bacteria in fermented products.
- Herbs and Flavorings: Fresh herbs, garlic, and spices can be added to butters and cheeses for customized flavors.

Safety and Hygiene in Dairy Processing

Working with milk and its derivatives requires strict attention to safety and hygiene. Dairy products are highly perishable and can harbor harmful bacteria if not handled properly.

- Cleanliness: Always start with clean equipment and work surfaces. Even small amounts of residue from previous cooking can contaminate milk and its derivatives. Regularly sterilize tools and containers, especially when making yogurt or cheese.
- Temperature Control: Keep milk and dairy products at the appropriate temperatures to prevent spoilage and bacterial growth. Use a thermometer to monitor temperatures during pasteurization, fermentation, and cooling.
- Proper Storage: Store milk and milk derivatives in airtight containers to prevent contamination and extend shelf life. Products like yogurt and cheese should be refrigerated immediately after preparation.

- Handling Raw Milk: If using raw milk, be aware of the increased risk of contamination. Raw milk should be pasteurized before use to ensure safety. If consuming or using raw milk, make sure it's from a reputable source and has been handled with care throughout its production and transportation.

By understanding these foundational processes and adhering to safety practices, you can confidently create a wide range of milk derivatives in your kitchen. Whether you're whipping up a batch of fresh cream, crafting artisanal butter, or venturing into the world of cheese-making, these basics will set you on the path to success.

Chapter 2: Fresh Creamy Delights

Homemade Cream: Whipping, Double, and Sour

Cream is a cornerstone of many delicious dishes, offering richness and texture that elevates both sweet and savory recipes. There are several types of cream you can make at home, each with distinct characteristics:

- Whipping Cream: This cream has a fat content of around 30-36%, making it ideal for whipping into soft peaks to top desserts or drinks. It adds a light, airy texture and a subtle richness to dishes.
- Double Cream: With a higher fat content of about 48%, double cream is thicker and richer than whipping cream. It's perfect for pouring over desserts, enriching sauces, or using as a base in custards and ganaches.
- Sour Cream: Made by fermenting cream with lactic acid bacteria, sour cream has a tangy flavor and thick consistency. It's commonly used in dips, toppings, and baking to add moisture and a slight tang.

Recipes
Classic Whipped Cream
Ingredients:

- 1 cup (240 ml) cold heavy whipping cream
- 2 tablespoons powdered sugar (optional)
- 1 teaspoon vanilla extract (optional)

Instructions:

1. Chill the Tools: Place the mixing bowl and whisk or beaters in the refrigerator for about 15 minutes. Cold tools help the cream whip more efficiently.

2. Whip the Cream: Pour the cold whipping cream into the chilled bowl. Begin whisking or using an electric mixer on medium speed.

3. Add Sweeteners and Flavoring: As the cream begins to thicken, add the powdered sugar and vanilla extract, if using. Continue to whip until soft peaks form. For stiffer peaks, whip a little longer, but be careful not to overwhip, or the cream will become grainy and eventually turn into butter.

4. Serve Immediately: Use the whipped cream as a topping for desserts like pies, cakes, or hot chocolate. It's best served fresh, but it can be stored in the refrigerator for up to 24 hours.

Sour Cream Dips and Toppings
Ingredients:
For Basic Sour Cream:

- 1 cup (240 ml) heavy cream
- 2 tablespoons buttermilk

For Dips and Toppings:

- 1 cup sour cream (homemade or store-bought)
- 1 tablespoon fresh lemon juice
- Salt and pepper to taste

Optional Add-ins:

- Chopped fresh herbs (chives, parsley, dill)
- Minced garlic

- Finely chopped green onions or shallots
- Spices like paprika, cumin, or cayenne pepper

Instructions:

Make the Sour Cream:

- Combine the heavy cream and buttermilk in a clean jar. Stir well and cover with a lid.
- Let the mixture sit at room temperature for 24 hours, during which it will thicken and develop a tangy flavor.
- Once thickened, stir the cream, cover it, and refrigerate it for another 24 hours before using.

Prepare Dips and Toppings:

- In a bowl, mix the sour cream with lemon juice, salt, and pepper to taste.
- Customize the flavor by adding chopped herbs, garlic, onions, or spices. Mix well.
- Serve as a dip for vegetables, chips, or as a topping for baked potatoes, tacos, or chili.
- Storage: Store any leftover sour cream or prepared dips in an airtight container in the refrigerator for up to a week.

Creamy Soups and Sauces
Ingredients:

- 1 cup (240 ml) double cream or heavy cream
- 2 tablespoons unsalted butter
- 1 small onion, finely chopped
- 2 cloves garlic, minced
- 2 tablespoons all-purpose flour
- 4 cups (960 ml) chicken or vegetable broth

- Salt and pepper to taste
- Optional Add-ins:
- Fresh herbs like thyme, parsley, or basil
- Grated cheese (parmesan, cheddar)
- Cooked vegetables (mushrooms, carrots, potatoes)
- Cooked meat (shredded chicken, bacon)

Instructions:

Sauté the Aromatics:

- In a large saucepan, melt the butter over medium heat. Add the chopped onion and garlic, cooking until they are soft and translucent.

Create the Base:

- Sprinkle the flour over the onion and garlic mixture, stirring constantly to create a roux. Cook for about 2 minutes to eliminate the raw flour taste.

Add the Broth:

- Gradually whisk in the broth, ensuring there are no lumps. Bring the mixture to a simmer, stirring frequently until it begins to thicken.

Incorporate the Cream:

- Reduce the heat to low and slowly pour in the cream, stirring to combine. Allow the soup or sauce to simmer for another 10 minutes, stirring occasionally.

Season and Enhance:

- Season with salt and pepper to taste. Add any optional ingredients like fresh herbs, cheese, or cooked vegetables or meat to enhance the flavor and texture.

Serve:

- Use the creamy base as a soup, or serve it over pasta, vegetables, or meats as a rich and flavorful sauce.
- Storage: Leftover soups or sauces can be stored in the refrigerator for up to 3 days. Reheat gently over low heat, adding a splash of broth or cream if necessary to thin it out.

These recipes showcase the richness and versatility of homemade cream, whether it's whipped into airy peaks, turned into tangy sour cream, or blended into comforting soups and sauces. Each preparation highlights the creamy indulgence that milk can bring to your culinary creations.

Chapter 3: Butter: From Churn to Table

Making Butter at Home: Salted, Unsalted, and Clarified

Butter is a staple ingredient in kitchens worldwide, prized for its rich flavor and versatility. Making butter at home is a simple yet rewarding process that allows you to control the quality and customize the taste. There are three primary types of butter you can create: salted, unsalted, and clarified.

- Salted Butter: Salted butter is made by adding salt to the butter after it has been churned. The salt acts as a preservative and enhances the flavor, making it ideal for spreading on bread and for general cooking.
- Unsalted Butter: Unsalted butter is pure butterfat without any added salt. It has a sweeter, creamier taste and is often preferred in baking where precise control over salt levels is important.
- Clarified Butter (Ghee): Clarified butter, or ghee, is made by slowly melting butter and allowing the water to evaporate and the milk solids to separate. The result is a pure butterfat that has a higher smoke point and a longer shelf life, making it perfect for frying and sautéing.

Recipes
Traditional Buttermilk Biscuits
Ingredients:

- 2 cups (250 g) all-purpose flour
- 1 tablespoon baking powder
- 1/2 teaspoon baking soda
- 1/2 teaspoon salt
- 6 tablespoons (85 g) unsalted butter, cold and cut into small cubes

- 3/4 cup (180 ml) buttermilk (use the leftover buttermilk from butter-making)
- Optional: 1 tablespoon sugar (for a slightly sweet biscuit)

Instructions:

1. Preheat the Oven: Preheat your oven to 450°F (230°C). Line a baking sheet with parchment paper.
2. Mix Dry Ingredients: In a large mixing bowl, whisk together the flour, baking powder, baking soda, and salt (and sugar if using).
3. Cut in the Butter: Add the cold, cubed butter to the flour mixture. Using a pastry cutter or your fingers, work the butter into the flour until the mixture resembles coarse crumbs. The butter pieces should be about the size of peas.
4. Add the Buttermilk: Pour in the buttermilk and gently stir until the dough begins to come together. Be careful not to overmix; the dough should be slightly shaggy and sticky.
5. Shape the Dough: Turn the dough out onto a floured surface and gently pat it into a rectangle about 1/2-inch (1.25 cm) thick. Fold the dough in half and gently pat it down again. Repeat this folding process two more times to create flaky layers.
6. Cut the Biscuits: Using a biscuit cutter or the rim of a glass, cut out biscuits from the dough. Place them on the prepared baking sheet, leaving a bit of space between each one.
7. Bake: Bake in the preheated oven for 10-12 minutes, or until the biscuits are golden brown on top.
8. Serve: Enjoy the biscuits warm, with a pat of homemade butter or a drizzle of honey. They are perfect for breakfast or as a side to soups and stews.

Herb-Infused Compound Butters
Ingredients:

- 1/2 cup (115 g) unsalted butter, softened
- 1 tablespoon fresh herbs, finely chopped (such as parsley, thyme, rosemary, or chives)
- 1/2 teaspoon garlic, minced (optional)
- 1/2 teaspoon lemon zest (optional)
- Salt and pepper to taste

Instructions:

1. Prepare the Butter: In a small mixing bowl, combine the softened butter with the chopped herbs. If using, add the minced garlic and lemon zest. Mix well until the herbs and seasonings are evenly distributed throughout the butter.
2. Season: Add salt and pepper to taste. Continue mixing until all ingredients are fully incorporated.
3. Shape the Butter: Transfer the butter mixture to a sheet of plastic wrap or parchment paper. Shape it into a log, twisting the ends of the wrap to seal. Alternatively, you can press the butter into a small ramekin or mold for a different presentation.
4. Chill: Refrigerate the butter for at least 1 hour to allow the flavors to meld and the butter to firm up.
5. Serve: Slice the compound butter and serve over grilled meats, fish, vegetables, or spread it on warm bread. Herb-infused butter adds a burst of flavor and elegance to any dish.
6. Storage: Store leftover compound butter in the refrigerator for up to two weeks, or freeze for up to three months.

Ghee: The Clarified Gold
Ingredients:

- 1 pound (450 g) unsalted butter

Instructions:

1. Melt the Butter: Place the butter in a heavy-bottomed saucepan over medium-low heat. Allow the butter to melt slowly. As it melts, it will separate into three layers: foam on top, clear butterfat in the middle, and milk solids on the bottom.
2. Simmer and Clarify: Once the butter has melted, reduce the heat to low. Let it simmer gently without stirring. The milk solids will begin to brown and sink to the bottom, while the foam will rise to the top.
3. Skim the Foam: Use a spoon to carefully skim off the foam from the surface of the butter. Continue simmering until the butter is clear and golden, and the milk solids have turned a light brown color. This process takes about 20-30 minutes.
4. Strain the Ghee: Line a fine mesh strainer with cheesecloth and place it over a clean jar or container. Pour the clarified butter through the strainer to remove the milk solids. Be sure to leave any browned bits at the bottom of the pan.
5. Cool and Store: Let the ghee cool to room temperature before sealing the jar. Ghee can be stored at room temperature in an airtight container for several months or in the refrigerator for even longer.
6. Use: Ghee's high smoke point makes it ideal for frying, sautéing, and roasting. Its nutty flavor adds depth to both sweet and savory dishes.

These butter recipes highlight the diverse ways butter can be used and enhanced in the kitchen. From the flaky, tender layers of traditional buttermilk biscuits to the aromatic allure of herb-infused compound butters, and the golden, clarified richness of ghee, each preparation showcases butter's unique ability to elevate everyday dishes to extraordinary heights.

Chapter 4: Cheese: Crafting Curd to Perfection

Introduction to Cheese-Making: Soft, Semi-Hard, and Hard Cheeses

Cheese-making is an ancient craft that transforms simple milk into a wide variety of textures and flavors, from soft, fresh cheeses to hard, aged varieties. The process involves coagulating the milk, separating the curds from the whey, and then shaping, salting, and aging the curds into cheese. The type of cheese produced depends on factors such as the type of milk used, the cultures and rennet added, and the techniques employed during the process.

- Soft Cheeses: These cheeses have a high moisture content and are often enjoyed fresh. They are typically mild in flavor with a creamy texture. Examples include mozzarella, ricotta, and paneer.
- Semi-Hard Cheeses: These cheeses have a firmer texture and can be aged for a few weeks to several months. They develop more complex flavors and can range from mild to sharp. Examples include gouda and havarti.
- Hard Cheeses: Hard cheeses are aged the longest, often for several months to years. They have a low moisture content, a dense texture, and a strong, sharp flavor. Cheddar and parmesan are classic examples.

Recipes
Fresh Mozzarella
Ingredients:

- 1 gallon (3.8 liters) whole milk, not ultra-pasteurized
- 1 1/2 teaspoons citric acid, dissolved in 1/4 cup (60 ml) cool

water

- 1/4 teaspoon liquid rennet, dissolved in 1/4 cup (60 ml) cool water
- 1 teaspoon salt

Instructions:

1. Prepare the Milk: Pour the milk into a large, non-reactive pot. Add the dissolved citric acid and stir gently to combine. Heat the milk over medium-low heat, slowly bringing it up to 90°F (32°C).

2. Add the Rennet: Once the milk reaches 90°F (32°C), remove it from the heat. Stir in the dissolved rennet using an up-and-down motion with your spoon. Cover the pot and let it sit undisturbed for 5-10 minutes, until the milk sets into a soft curd.

3. Cut the Curds: Once the curd has formed, use a long knife to cut it into 1-inch (2.5 cm) cubes. Let the curds rest for 5 minutes to firm up.

4. Heat and Stir the Curds: Place the pot back on low heat and gently stir the curds, bringing the temperature up to 105°F (40°C). Keep stirring for 5-10 minutes until the curds become slightly firmer and separate more from the whey.

5. Drain the Whey: Using a slotted spoon, transfer the curds to a microwave-safe bowl, draining off as much whey as possible. Microwave the curds on high for 1 minute.

6. Stretch the Mozzarella: After microwaving, knead and stretch the curds with your hands (wear gloves if it's too hot). If the curds cool down too much, microwave them for an additional 30 seconds. Continue stretching until the curds are smooth and shiny. Add salt and knead it into the cheese.

7. Shape and Chill: Shape the mozzarella into a ball or log. Place it in a bowl of cool water for 5 minutes, then transfer it to an ice

water bath to firm up for another 10 minutes.

8. Serve: Fresh mozzarella is best enjoyed the same day, but it can be stored in the refrigerator for up to a week in a brine or wrapped in plastic.

Ricotta and Paneer

Ingredients:

- 1 gallon (3.8 liters) whole milk, not ultra-pasteurized
- 1/4 cup (60 ml) fresh lemon juice or white vinegar
- 1 teaspoon salt (for ricotta)

Instructions:

1. Heat the Milk: Pour the milk into a large pot and slowly heat it over medium heat until it reaches 185°F (85°C). Stir occasionally to prevent scorching.
2. Add the Acid: Once the milk reaches the desired temperature, remove it from the heat and slowly stir in the lemon juice or vinegar. The milk will begin to curdle immediately, forming curds and whey.
3. Let it Sit: Allow the mixture to sit undisturbed for 10-15 minutes to ensure full curd formation.

Drain the Curds:

- For Ricotta: Line a colander with cheesecloth and place it over a large bowl. Gently ladle the curds into the colander, allowing the whey to drain off. For a creamier ricotta, drain for about 10-15 minutes. For a firmer texture, drain for up to 30 minutes. Add salt to taste and stir gently.
- For Paneer: Line the colander with cheesecloth, pour in the curds, and gather the cheesecloth corners to form a bundle. Press out excess whey, then place a heavy weight on top to

press the paneer for 30-60 minutes, depending on the desired firmness.

Serve:

- Ricotta: Use ricotta in lasagna, on toast, or in desserts like cannoli or cheesecake. Store in the refrigerator for up to 3 days.
- Paneer: Cut the paneer into cubes and use it in Indian dishes like palak paneer or paneer tikka. Store in the refrigerator for up to 5 days.

Aged Cheddar
Ingredients:

- 2 gallons (7.6 liters) whole milk, not ultra-pasteurized
- 1 packet mesophilic culture
- 1/2 teaspoon liquid rennet, dissolved in 1/4 cup (60 ml) cool water
- 1 tablespoon salt

Instructions:

1. Prepare the Milk: Pour the milk into a large pot and heat it to 85°F (29°C). Sprinkle the mesophilic culture over the milk and let it rehydrate for 2 minutes, then stir it in thoroughly.
2. Add the Rennet: Stir in the dissolved rennet using an up-and-down motion. Cover the pot and let the milk sit undisturbed at 85°F (29°C) for about 45 minutes, or until a clean break is achieved when you insert a knife into the curd.
3. Cut the Curds: Cut the curds into 1/2-inch (1.25 cm) cubes and let them rest for 5 minutes.
4. Cook the Curds: Slowly heat the curds to 100°F (38°C), stirring gently to prevent matting. Maintain this temperature for 30 minutes, stirring occasionally.

5. Drain and Cheddar the Curds: Drain the whey from the curds and place the curds in a cheesecloth-lined mold. Press the curds under 10 pounds (4.5 kg) of weight for 10 minutes. Remove, flip the curds, and press under 20 pounds (9 kg) for 12 hours.

6. Salt and Age the Cheese: After pressing, remove the cheese from the mold and rub salt on all sides. Let the cheese air-dry at room temperature for 2-3 days, turning it regularly. Once dry, wax or vacuum seal the cheese and age it in a cool, humid environment (ideally 50-55°F or 10-13°C) for 3-12 months, flipping it weekly.

7. Serve: Once aged to your preference, unwrap the cheddar, slice, and enjoy its sharp, tangy flavor. Store in the refrigerator, tightly wrapped, for up to a month.

These cheese recipes provide a journey through the cheese-making process, from the soft, milky richness of fresh mozzarella and ricotta to the firmer, more complex flavors of aged cheddar. Each recipe offers a different aspect of cheese-making, allowing you to experiment and appreciate the art of crafting curds to perfection.

Chapter 5: Yogurt: Cultured and Creamy

The Science Behind Yogurt: Fermentation and Probiotics

Yogurt is a beloved dairy product with roots in ancient cultures, praised for its tangy flavor and health benefits. The process of making yogurt hinges on fermentation, where beneficial bacteria convert the lactose in milk into lactic acid. This acid not only thickens the milk but also gives yogurt its characteristic tartness. The most common bacteria used in yogurt-making are Lactobacillus bulgaricus and Streptococcus thermophilus, though other probiotic strains may be included for additional health benefits.

Probiotics, the live bacteria present in yogurt, play a significant role in promoting gut health. These beneficial microorganisms help balance the gut microbiome, aid digestion, and can boost the immune system. Making yogurt at home allows you to control the ingredients and ensure a rich, probiotic-packed final product.

Recipes

Greek Yogurt at Home

Ingredients:

- 1 gallon (3.8 liters) whole milk
- 1/4 cup (60 ml) plain yogurt with live active cultures (as a starter)
- Optional: 1/4 cup (60 ml) powdered milk (for thicker yogurt)

Instructions:

1. Heat the Milk: Pour the milk into a large, heavy-bottomed pot and heat it over medium heat until it reaches 180°F (82°C). Stir occasionally to prevent the milk from scorching. This step helps denature the proteins and results in a thicker yogurt.
2. Cool the Milk: Remove the pot from the heat and allow the

milk to cool to 110°F (43°C). To speed up cooling, you can place the pot in a sink filled with cold water, stirring the milk gently.

3. Inoculate the Milk: Once the milk has cooled to 110°F (43°C), stir in the plain yogurt with live cultures (and powdered milk, if using) until fully dissolved.

4. Incubate: Pour the inoculated milk into a large, clean container or individual jars. Cover the container(s) with a lid or plastic wrap. Keep the yogurt warm at around 110°F (43°C) for 6-12 hours to allow fermentation. You can use a yogurt maker, an oven with the light on, or a warm spot in your kitchen. The longer the fermentation, the tangier the yogurt will be.

5. Strain for Greek Yogurt: Once the yogurt has set, it's ready to eat as is, but for Greek yogurt, you'll need to strain it. Line a colander with cheesecloth and place it over a large bowl. Pour the yogurt into the colander and let it drain for 2-4 hours, depending on your desired thickness.

6. Store and Serve: Transfer the strained Greek yogurt to an airtight container and refrigerate. It will keep for up to 2 weeks. Enjoy it plain, with honey, or topped with fruit.

7. Flavored Yogurts: Fruit, Honey, and Vanilla

Ingredients:

- 2 cups (480 ml) Greek yogurt (from the recipe above)
- 1/4 cup (60 ml) honey or maple syrup
- 1 teaspoon pure vanilla extract
- 1 cup (150 g) fresh or frozen fruit, chopped (e.g., berries, mango, peaches)

Instructions:

1. Prepare the Base: In a medium bowl, whisk together the Greek

yogurt, honey or maple syrup, and vanilla extract until smooth and well combined.

2. Add the Fruit: Stir in the chopped fruit of your choice. If using frozen fruit, let it thaw slightly before mixing. The fruit will release juices that naturally sweeten and flavor the yogurt.

3. Serve: Divide the flavored yogurt into bowls or jars. It's ready to enjoy immediately, or you can refrigerate it for up to 5 days.

4. Variations:

- For a layered parfait, alternate layers of flavored yogurt with granola and additional fruit.
- Create a swirled effect by adding a spoonful of fruit preserves or compote and lightly swirling it through the yogurt.

Savory Yogurt Dips and Marinades
Savory Yogurt Dip
Ingredients:

- 2 cups (480 ml) Greek yogurt
- 1 clove garlic, minced
- 1 tablespoon lemon juice
- 1 tablespoon olive oil
- 1 teaspoon ground cumin
- 1/2 teaspoon paprika
- Salt and pepper to taste
- 2 tablespoons fresh herbs, chopped (e.g., mint, dill, or parsley)

Instructions:

1. Mix the Ingredients: In a medium bowl, combine the Greek yogurt, minced garlic, lemon juice, olive oil, cumin, and paprika. Stir until well blended.

2. Season: Add salt and pepper to taste. Stir in the chopped herbs for added freshness and flavor.

3. Chill and Serve: Refrigerate the dip for at least 30 minutes before serving to allow the flavors to meld. Serve with fresh vegetables, pita bread, or as a sauce for grilled meats.

Yogurt Marinade
Ingredients:

- 1 cup (240 ml) Greek yogurt
- 2 tablespoons olive oil
- 2 tablespoons lemon juice
- 1 tablespoon grated ginger
- 2 cloves garlic, minced
- 1 teaspoon ground coriander
- 1 teaspoon ground cumin
- 1/2 teaspoon turmeric
- Salt and pepper to taste

Instructions:

1. Combine the Ingredients: In a large bowl, whisk together the Greek yogurt, olive oil, lemon juice, ginger, garlic, coriander, cumin, and turmeric.
2. Season: Add salt and pepper to taste. Stir until the marinade is smooth and well combined.
3. Marinate the Meat: Add your choice of meat (chicken, lamb, or beef) to the bowl, making sure each piece is well coated with the marinade. Cover and refrigerate for at least 2 hours, or overnight for the best flavor.
4. Cook and Serve: Grill, bake, or sauté the marinated meat until fully cooked. The yogurt marinade will tenderize the meat while infusing it with rich, aromatic flavors.

These yogurt recipes showcase the versatility of yogurt beyond its traditional uses. Whether you're crafting thick, creamy Greek yogurt, experimenting with fresh fruit and natural sweeteners for flavored variations, or using yogurt as a base for savory dips and marinades, you'll discover how yogurt can enhance both sweet and savory dishes alike.

Chapter 6: Indulgent Desserts with Milk Derivatives

Using Milk Derivatives in Desserts: Custards, Puddings, and Ice Creams

Milk derivatives are the foundation of many indulgent desserts, providing richness, creaminess, and a smooth texture that elevates simple ingredients into luxurious treats. Custards, puddings, and ice creams are classic examples where milk, cream, and eggs come together to create decadent flavors and textures. Whether it's the creamy consistency of a well-made custard, the silky smoothness of a pudding, or the rich, velvety texture of ice cream, these desserts highlight the versatility and indulgence that milk derivatives offer.

Recipes

Classic Vanilla Ice Cream

Ingredients:

- 2 cups (480 ml) heavy cream
- 1 cup (240 ml) whole milk
- 3/4 cup (150 g) granulated sugar
- 1 vanilla bean, split and seeds scraped (or 2 teaspoons pure vanilla extract)
- 4 large egg yolks

Instructions:

1. Prepare the Base: In a medium saucepan, combine the heavy cream, whole milk, and sugar. Add the vanilla bean seeds and the split pod (if using vanilla extract, add it later). Heat the mixture over medium heat, stirring occasionally, until the sugar is fully dissolved and the mixture is hot but not boiling.
2. Temper the Egg Yolks: In a separate bowl, whisk the egg yolks

until smooth. Gradually pour about 1/2 cup of the hot cream mixture into the egg yolks, whisking constantly to temper them. This prevents the eggs from curdling when added to the hot liquid.

3. Cook the Custard: Pour the tempered egg yolks back into the saucepan with the remaining cream mixture. Cook over medium-low heat, stirring constantly with a wooden spoon, until the mixture thickens enough to coat the back of the spoon (170-175°F or 77-80°C). Do not let it boil.

4. Chill the Custard: Remove the custard from the heat and strain it through a fine-mesh sieve into a clean bowl to remove any cooked egg bits and the vanilla pod. Stir in the vanilla extract if using. Cover the bowl with plastic wrap, pressing it directly onto the surface of the custard to prevent a skin from forming. Refrigerate until completely chilled, at least 4 hours or overnight.

5. Churn the Ice Cream: Once the custard is chilled, pour it into an ice cream maker and churn according to the manufacturer's instructions, usually 20-25 minutes, until the ice cream reaches a soft-serve consistency.

6. Freeze the Ice Cream: Transfer the ice cream to an airtight container, cover, and freeze for at least 4 hours or until firm. Enjoy your classic vanilla ice cream as is, or use it as a base for mix-ins like chocolate chips, fruit, or nuts.

Rich Chocolate Pudding
Ingredients:

- 2 cups (480 ml) whole milk
- 1/2 cup (100 g) granulated sugar
- 1/4 cup (30 g) unsweetened cocoa powder
- 2 tablespoons cornstarch
- 1/4 teaspoon salt

- 3 large egg yolks
- 4 oz (115 g) semi-sweet chocolate, chopped
- 2 tablespoons unsalted butter
- 1 teaspoon pure vanilla extract

Instructions:

1. Mix the Dry Ingredients: In a medium saucepan, whisk together the sugar, cocoa powder, cornstarch, and salt.
2. Add the Milk and Cook: Gradually whisk in the milk until smooth. Place the saucepan over medium heat and cook, whisking constantly, until the mixture begins to bubble and thicken, about 5-7 minutes.
3. Temper the Egg Yolks: In a separate bowl, whisk the egg yolks. Slowly pour about 1/2 cup of the hot cocoa mixture into the egg yolks, whisking constantly to prevent curdling. Return the tempered egg yolks to the saucepan.
4. Cook Until Thickened: Continue to cook the mixture, whisking constantly, until it thickens further, about 2-3 minutes. The pudding should be thick enough to coat the back of a spoon.
5. Add the Chocolate and Butter: Remove the saucepan from the heat and whisk in the chopped chocolate, butter, and vanilla extract until smooth and glossy.
6. Chill and Serve: Pour the pudding into individual serving dishes or a large bowl. Cover with plastic wrap, pressing it directly onto the surface to prevent a skin from forming. Chill in the refrigerator for at least 2 hours before serving. Top with whipped cream or shaved chocolate for an extra indulgent touch.

Crème Brûlée

Ingredients:

- 2 cups (480 ml) heavy cream
- 1 vanilla bean, split and seeds scraped (or 1 teaspoon pure vanilla extract)
- 5 large egg yolks
- 1/2 cup (100 g) granulated sugar, plus extra for topping
- Pinch of salt

Instructions:

1. Preheat the Oven: Preheat your oven to 325°F (163°C). Place 4-6 ramekins in a baking dish with high sides.
2. Heat the Cream: In a medium saucepan, combine the heavy cream, vanilla bean seeds, and split pod (or vanilla extract). Heat over medium heat until the cream is hot but not boiling. Remove from heat and let it steep for a few minutes.
3. Mix the Egg Yolks: In a separate bowl, whisk together the egg yolks, sugar, and salt until the mixture is pale and thick.
4. Temper the Egg Yolks: Slowly pour the hot cream into the egg yolk mixture, whisking constantly to prevent the eggs from cooking. Strain the mixture through a fine-mesh sieve to remove any cooked egg bits and the vanilla pod.
5. Fill the Ramekins: Divide the custard mixture evenly among the ramekins. Pour hot water into the baking dish, filling it halfway up the sides of the ramekins to create a water bath.
6. Bake: Carefully transfer the baking dish to the oven and bake for 40-45 minutes, or until the custards are set but still slightly jiggly in the center.
7. Chill the Custards: Remove the ramekins from the water bath and let them cool to room temperature. Then refrigerate for at least 4 hours or overnight.
8. Caramelize the Sugar: Just before serving, sprinkle a thin, even layer of granulated sugar over each custard. Using a kitchen torch, caramelize the sugar until it forms a crisp, golden-brown

crust. If you don't have a torch, you can place the ramekins under a broiler for a few minutes, watching carefully to avoid burning.

9. Serve: Allow the caramelized sugar to harden for a minute before serving. Enjoy cracking through the crisp sugar crust to reveal the smooth, creamy custard beneath.

These recipes showcase the versatility and indulgence that milk derivatives bring to desserts. Whether you're savoring the timeless elegance of a crème brûlée, the comforting richness of chocolate pudding, or the refreshing delight of homemade vanilla ice cream, these desserts are a celebration of dairy's ability to transform simple ingredients into decadent treats.

Chapter 7: Milk Powders and Condensed Milks

Powdered Milk vs. Condensed Milk: Uses and Benefits
Powdered Milk:
Powdered milk is dried milk with all the moisture removed. It's a versatile ingredient that can be reconstituted with water to use as liquid milk or utilized in recipes as a dry ingredient. Its benefits include a long shelf life, convenience, and ease of storage.

Uses:

- Baking: Enhances the richness of baked goods like bread and cookies.
- Reconstitution: Can be mixed with water to make liquid milk.
- Emergency Stock: Ideal for situations where fresh milk isn't available.

Condensed Milk:
Condensed milk is made by removing most of the water from milk and adding sugar, resulting in a thick, sweet product. It's often used in desserts due to its rich flavor and creamy texture.

Uses:

- Desserts: Essential for recipes such as pies, caramel, and sweets.
- Sweetener: Adds sweetness and creaminess to various dishes.
- Flavor Enhancer: Ideal for both cold and baked goods.

Recipes
Instant Hot Cocoa Mix
Ingredients:

- 1 cup (120 g) powdered milk
- 1 cup (120 g) unsweetened cocoa powder

- 1/2 cup (100 g) granulated sugar
- 1/4 cup (60 g) powdered sugar
- 1/2 teaspoon salt
- 1/2 teaspoon vanilla powder (optional)

Instructions:

1. Mix Ingredients: In a large bowl, combine powdered milk, unsweetened cocoa powder, granulated sugar, powdered sugar, salt, and vanilla powder (if using). Whisk until evenly mixed.
2. Store: Transfer the mixture to an airtight container or jar. Store in a cool, dry place for up to 6 months.
3. Prepare Hot Cocoa: To make a cup of hot cocoa, stir 1/4 cup of the mix into 1 cup of hot water or milk. Stir until completely dissolved. Adjust the amount of mix to your taste preference.
4. Serve: Enjoy with a topping of whipped cream or marshmallows if desired.

Dulce de Leche
Ingredients:

- 1 can (14 oz or 397 g) sweetened condensed milk

Instructions:

1. Heat Method: Pour the sweetened condensed milk into a heavy-bottomed saucepan. Cook over medium-low heat, stirring constantly to prevent burning, for about 1-1.5 hours, or until the mixture thickens and turns a caramel color.
2. Cool and Store: Remove from heat and let it cool to room temperature. Store in an airtight container in the refrigerator for up to 2 weeks.
3. Serve: Use as a topping for ice cream, pancakes, or as a filling for cakes and pastries.

Fudge and Caramel
Fudge
Ingredients:

- 1 can (14 oz or 397 g) sweetened condensed milk
- 2 cups (400 g) granulated sugar
- 1/2 cup (115 g) unsalted butter
- 1 cup (240 ml) milk
- 1 teaspoon vanilla extract
- Pinch of salt

Instructions:

1. Prepare Ingredients: Line an 8-inch (20 cm) square baking pan with parchment paper.
2. Cook the Mixture: In a heavy-bottomed saucepan, combine the sweetened condensed milk, sugar, butter, and milk. Cook over medium heat, stirring constantly, until the mixture reaches 234°F (112°C) on a candy thermometer.
3. Add Vanilla: Remove from heat and stir in the vanilla extract and a pinch of salt. Continue to stir for 1-2 minutes until the mixture starts to thicken.
4. Pour and Set: Pour the fudge mixture into the prepared pan, spreading it evenly. Let it cool to room temperature before cutting into squares.

Caramel
Ingredients:

- 1 cup (200 g) granulated sugar
- 6 tablespoons (85 g) unsalted butter
- 1/2 cup (120 ml) heavy cream
- Pinch of salt

Instructions:

1. Cook Sugar: In a medium saucepan over medium heat, melt the granulated sugar, stirring constantly until it turns a deep amber color. Be careful not to burn it.
2. Add Butter: Once the sugar is melted, add the butter and stir until fully incorporated. The mixture will bubble up, so be cautious.
3. Add Cream: Gradually pour in the heavy cream while continuing to stir. Cook for another minute or two, until the caramel is smooth and thickened.
4. Cool and Store: Remove from heat and stir in a pinch of salt. Let the caramel cool slightly before transferring it to a jar. Store in the refrigerator for up to 2 weeks.
5. Serve: Drizzle over ice cream, use as a filling for candies, or enjoy with fresh fruit.

These recipes highlight the diverse applications of powdered milk and condensed milk, from rich and creamy hot cocoa to luscious caramel and fudge. Each uses milk derivatives to create delicious, comforting desserts that are perfect for any occasion.

Chapter 8: Sauces, Dips, and Spreads

Enhancing Dishes with Milk-Based Sauces

Milk-based sauces are essential in many cuisines for adding creaminess, richness, and flavor to dishes. These sauces can transform simple ingredients into gourmet meals. Whether you're making a classic béchamel for a lasagna, a flavorful Mornay sauce for gratins, or a creamy Alfredo sauce for pasta, milk-based sauces enhance dishes with their velvety textures and rich flavors. Additionally, cream cheese spreads are versatile for dips, sandwiches, and appetizers.

Recipes

Béchamel Sauce

Ingredients:

- 4 tablespoons (55 g) unsalted butter
- 1/4 cup (30 g) all-purpose flour
- 2 cups (480 ml) whole milk
- 1/4 teaspoon salt
- 1/4 teaspoon ground white pepper
- 1/4 teaspoon ground nutmeg (optional)

Instructions:

1. Melt Butter: In a medium saucepan, melt the butter over medium heat until bubbly but not browned.
2. Add Flour: Whisk in the flour and cook for about 1-2 minutes, stirring constantly, to form a smooth roux. The mixture should be slightly golden but not dark.
3. Add Milk: Gradually pour in the milk while whisking constantly to avoid lumps. Continue to cook and whisk until the sauce thickens and comes to a gentle simmer, about 5-7 minutes.

4. Season: Stir in the salt, white pepper, and nutmeg if using. Continue to cook for an additional minute, then remove from heat.
5. Serve or Store: Use immediately in your recipe or let cool before storing in an airtight container in the refrigerator for up to 3 days. Reheat gently before using.

Mornay Sauce
Ingredients:

- 2 cups (480 ml) béchamel sauce (see recipe above)
- 1 cup (100 g) grated Gruyère cheese
- 1/2 cup (50 g) grated Parmesan cheese
- 1/4 teaspoon ground white pepper
- 1/4 teaspoon ground nutmeg

Instructions:

1. Prepare Béchamel: Start with 2 cups of prepared béchamel sauce.
2. Add Cheese: Heat the béchamel sauce over medium-low heat. Gradually stir in the Gruyère and Parmesan cheeses until melted and smooth.
3. Season: Add the white pepper and nutmeg, stirring to combine.
4. Serve or Store: Use the sauce immediately over vegetables, gratins, or pasta, or store in an airtight container in the refrigerator for up to 3 days. Reheat gently before using.

Cream Cheese Spread Variations
Classic Cream Cheese Spread
Ingredients:

- 8 oz (225 g) cream cheese, softened
- 1/4 cup (60 ml) sour cream

- 2 tablespoons chopped fresh chives
- 1 clove garlic, minced
- Salt and pepper to taste

Instructions:

1. Combine Ingredients: In a bowl, mix together the softened cream cheese and sour cream until smooth.
2. Add Flavorings: Stir in the chives, garlic, salt, and pepper until evenly distributed.
3. Chill: Refrigerate for at least 30 minutes to allow the flavors to meld.
4. Serve: Use as a dip for vegetables, a spread for bagels, or as a filling for sandwiches.

Herbed Cream Cheese Spread
Ingredients:

- 8 oz (225 g) cream cheese, softened
- 1/4 cup (60 ml) sour cream
- 2 tablespoons finely chopped fresh basil
- 2 tablespoons finely chopped fresh parsley
- 1 tablespoon finely chopped fresh dill
- 1 teaspoon lemon juice
- Salt and pepper to taste

Instructions:

1. Mix Base: In a bowl, combine the softened cream cheese and sour cream until smooth.
2. Add Herbs: Stir in the basil, parsley, dill, and lemon juice.
3. Season: Add salt and pepper to taste.
4. Chill: Refrigerate for at least 30 minutes before serving.
5. Serve: Perfect as a dip for crackers or vegetables, or as a spread

for sandwiches and wraps.

Alfredo Sauce
Ingredients:

- 1/2 cup (115 g) unsalted butter
- 1 cup (240 ml) heavy cream
- 1 cup (100 g) grated Parmesan cheese
- 2 cloves garlic, minced
- 1/4 teaspoon salt
- 1/4 teaspoon ground black pepper
- 1/4 teaspoon ground nutmeg (optional)

Instructions:

1. Melt Butter: In a large skillet over medium heat, melt the butter until it begins to bubble.
2. Add Garlic: Add the minced garlic and cook for about 1 minute, until fragrant.
3. Add Cream: Pour in the heavy cream and bring to a gentle simmer, cooking for about 2-3 minutes.
4. Add Cheese: Gradually stir in the Parmesan cheese until the sauce is smooth and thickened.
5. Season: Stir in the salt, black pepper, and nutmeg if using.
6. Serve: Toss the sauce with cooked pasta or vegetables, or use it as a topping for baked dishes.
7. Store: Refrigerate leftovers in an airtight container for up to 3 days. Reheat gently before serving.

These recipes showcase the versatility and richness of milk-based sauces, dips, and spreads. From the classic creamy béchamel and indulgent Alfredo sauce to versatile cream cheese spreads, these recipes are perfect for enhancing a variety of dishes with delicious, dairy-rich flavors.

Chapter 9: Cow's Milk in Global Cuisine

Exploring International Dishes with Milk Derivatives

Cow's milk plays a vital role in many global cuisines, offering diverse and flavorful ways to enjoy dairy. From the creamy curries of India to the indulgent desserts of Italy and the elegant French appetizers, milk derivatives enhance these dishes with their unique textures and rich flavors. This chapter explores three iconic recipes from around the world, highlighting how cow's milk derivatives are celebrated in different culinary traditions.

Recipes

Indian Paneer Curry

Ingredients:

For the Paneer:

- 4 cups (1 liter) whole milk
- 2 tablespoons lemon juice or vinegar

For the Curry:

- 2 tablespoons vegetable oil
- 1 large onion, finely chopped
- 2 cloves garlic, minced
- 1 tablespoon ginger, minced
- 2 large tomatoes, pureed
- 1 cup (240 ml) coconut milk
- 1/2 cup (120 ml) water
- 1 tablespoon ground coriander
- 1 tablespoon ground cumin
- 1 teaspoon turmeric powder
- 1 teaspoon garam masala
- 1/2 teaspoon red chili powder (adjust to taste)

- Salt to taste
- 1/2 cup (75 g) fresh cilantro, chopped

Instructions:

1. Make Paneer:

- Heat the milk in a large saucepan over medium heat until it starts to boil. Reduce the heat and add lemon juice or vinegar, stirring gently until the milk curdles.
- Remove from heat and pour the curdled milk into a cheesecloth-lined sieve. Rinse under cold water to remove the acidic taste. Gather the cloth and squeeze out excess liquid.
- Press the paneer under a heavy object for at least 1 hour to firm up.

1. Prepare the Curry:

- Heat vegetable oil in a large skillet over medium heat. Add chopped onion and sauté until golden brown.
- Add garlic and ginger, cooking for an additional minute until fragrant.
- Stir in the pureed tomatoes and cook for 5-7 minutes, until the oil separates from the mixture.
- Add coriander, cumin, turmeric, garam masala, red chili powder, and salt. Cook for another 2 minutes.
- Pour in coconut milk and water, stirring to combine. Simmer for 10 minutes to allow flavors to meld.
- Cut the paneer into cubes and add to the curry. Simmer for an additional 5 minutes.
- Garnish with fresh cilantro before serving.
- Serve: Enjoy hot with steamed rice or naan bread.

Italian Tiramisu
Ingredients:
For the Mascarpone Mixture:

- 1 cup (240 ml) heavy cream
- 8 oz (225 g) mascarpone cheese, softened
- 1/2 cup (100 g) granulated sugar
- 1 teaspoon vanilla extract
- 4 large egg yolks

For Assembly:

- **1 cup (240 ml) strong brewed coffee, cooled**
- **1/4 cup (60 ml) coffee liqueur (optional)**
- **24-30 ladyfingers**
- **Unsweetened cocoa powder for dusting**

Instructions:

1. Prepare the Mascarpone Mixture:

- In a large bowl, beat the heavy cream until soft peaks form.
- In a separate bowl, whisk together mascarpone cheese, sugar, and vanilla extract until smooth.
- In a third bowl, whisk the egg yolks until pale and creamy. Gently fold the mascarpone mixture into the egg yolks, followed by the whipped cream. Mix until well combined.

1. Assemble the Tiramisu:

- Combine the cooled coffee and coffee liqueur in a shallow dish.
- Quickly dip each ladyfinger into the coffee mixture, making sure not to soak them.
- Arrange a layer of dipped ladyfingers in the bottom of a serving

dish or individual cups.

- Spread half of the mascarpone mixture over the ladyfingers.
- Add another layer of dipped ladyfingers, followed by the remaining mascarpone mixture.

1. Chill and Serve:

- Refrigerate for at least 4 hours, or overnight for best results.
- Before serving, dust the top with unsweetened cocoa powder.

French Brie en Croûte
Ingredients:

- 1 round of Brie cheese (about 8 oz or 225 g)
- 1 sheet of puff pastry, thawed
- 1/4 cup (60 ml) fig jam or fruit preserves
- 1 egg, beaten (for egg wash)
- Fresh thyme sprigs or chopped nuts for garnish (optional)

Instructions:

1. Prepare the Cheese:

- Preheat the oven to 375°F (190°C).
- Roll out the puff pastry on a lightly floured surface to smooth any creases.

1. Assemble the Brie:

- Spread a thin layer of fig jam or fruit preserves over the top of the Brie cheese.
- Place the Brie in the center of the puff pastry sheet. Fold the pastry over the cheese, trimming any excess and sealing the edges with a bit of water.

- Brush the pastry with beaten egg to ensure a golden, shiny finish.

1. Bake:

- Place the wrapped Brie on a baking sheet lined with parchment paper.
- Bake for 20-25 minutes, or until the pastry is golden brown and puffed.

1. Serve:

- Let cool for a few minutes before serving. Garnish with fresh thyme or chopped nuts if desired.
- Serve warm with crackers or crusty bread.

These recipes showcase the diverse and delectable ways cow's milk derivatives are used in global cuisine. From the savory, spice-rich paneer curry of India to the creamy, coffee-soaked tiramisu of Italy and the elegant, baked Brie en Croûte of France, each dish highlights the versatility and indulgence that dairy brings to international flavors.

Chapter 10: Vegan Alternatives and Dairy-Free Options

Exploring Plant-Based Alternatives to Cow's Milk Derivatives

As more people embrace plant-based diets or seek dairy-free options due to allergies or dietary preferences, plant-based alternatives to cow's milk derivatives have become increasingly popular. These alternatives not only mimic the texture and flavor of traditional dairy products but also offer unique health benefits and versatility. This chapter explores three popular vegan alternatives: cashew cream, almond milk yogurt, and vegan butter, providing recipes to help you incorporate these dairy-free options into your cooking and baking.

Recipes

Cashew Cream

Ingredients:

- 1 cup (150 g) raw cashews, soaked
- 1/2 cup (120 ml) water (or more for desired consistency)
- 1 tablespoon lemon juice
- 1/2 teaspoon salt
- 1 tablespoon maple syrup or agave syrup (optional for sweetness)

Instructions:

1. Soak Cashews: Place the cashews in a bowl and cover with water. Soak for at least 4 hours or overnight. Drain and rinse.
2. Blend Ingredients: In a high-speed blender or food processor, combine the soaked cashews, 1/2 cup water, lemon juice, and salt. Blend until smooth and creamy. Add more water if needed to reach your desired consistency.
3. Sweeten (Optional): If you prefer a sweeter cream, blend in the

maple syrup or agave syrup.

4. Serve or Store: Use immediately as a topping for fruits, pancakes, or desserts, or store in an airtight container in the refrigerator for up to 5 days. It may thicken upon chilling; simply blend again with a little water to loosen.

Almond Milk Yogurt
Ingredients:

- 1 cup (240 ml) almond milk (unsweetened)
- 1 tablespoon cornstarch
- 2 tablespoons maple syrup or agave syrup
- 1/4 cup (60 ml) plain dairy-free yogurt (for starter culture)
- 1/2 teaspoon vanilla extract (optional)

Instructions:

1. Heat Almond Milk: In a saucepan, heat the almond milk over medium heat until it's warm but not boiling. Whisk in the cornstarch and cook until the milk thickens slightly, about 2-3 minutes.
2. Cool: Remove from heat and let the mixture cool to around 110°F (43°C), which is warm but not hot to the touch.
3. Add Sweetener and Starter: Stir in the maple syrup, plain dairy-free yogurt, and vanilla extract (if using). Mix well.
4. Incubate: Transfer the mixture to a clean jar or bowl, cover with a cloth, and place in a warm, draft-free area (such as an oven with the light on) for 6-12 hours, or until thickened and tangy.
5. Chill: Once thickened, refrigerate the yogurt for at least 4 hours before serving. Store in the refrigerator for up to 1 week.

Vegan Butter
Ingredients:

- 1/2 cup (120 ml) coconut oil, solidified
- 1/4 cup (60 ml) refined sunflower oil or light olive oil
- 1/4 cup (60 ml) unsweetened soy milk or almond milk
- 1 tablespoon nutritional yeast
- 1/2 teaspoon salt
- 1 teaspoon lemon juice

Instructions:

1. Combine Ingredients: In a bowl, mix the solidified coconut oil with the sunflower oil or light olive oil until well blended.
2. Add Milk: Slowly whisk in the soy milk or almond milk, mixing until smooth.
3. Flavor: Stir in the nutritional yeast, salt, and lemon juice until fully incorporated.
4. Chill: Pour the mixture into a container and refrigerate until firm, about 2 hours. The butter will firm up as it cools.
5. Serve: Use as you would regular butter for spreading, baking, or cooking. Store in the refrigerator for up to 2 weeks.

These vegan alternatives provide delicious, dairy-free options for those looking to replace traditional cow's milk derivatives. Whether you're making a creamy cashew sauce, tangy almond milk yogurt, or versatile vegan butter, these recipes offer plant-based solutions that cater to various dietary needs and preferences.

Chapter 11: Kefir and Other Fermented Beverages

The Benefits of Kefir and Fermented Milk Drinks

Fermented milk beverages like kefir, lassi, and ayran have been enjoyed for centuries across various cultures, not only for their refreshing taste but also for their numerous health benefits. These beverages are rich in probiotics, which promote gut health, aid digestion, and boost the immune system. This chapter explores the benefits of these fermented drinks and provides recipes for making traditional and flavored kefir, lassi variations, and the refreshing yogurt drink ayran.

The Benefits of Kefir and Fermented Milk Drinks

1. Probiotics and Gut Health:

- Kefir: Kefir is one of the most probiotic-rich foods available. It contains a diverse array of beneficial bacteria and yeast, which help balance the gut microbiome, improve digestion, and enhance nutrient absorption.
- Lassi and Ayran: Both lassi and ayran are rich in probiotics, although they have a slightly lower diversity of microorganisms compared to kefir. Regular consumption of these drinks can contribute to a healthy gut and support overall well-being.

2. Improved Digestion:

- The probiotics in kefir, lassi, and ayran aid in breaking down food more efficiently, reducing the likelihood of digestive discomfort, bloating, and constipation. They also help in the digestion of lactose, making these drinks suitable for some people who are lactose intolerant.

3. Enhanced Immune System:

- The beneficial bacteria in fermented milk beverages can help strengthen the immune system by stimulating the production of antibodies and promoting the activity of white blood cells. This makes kefir, lassi, and ayran valuable additions to a diet aimed at supporting immune health.

4. Nutrient-Rich:

- These drinks are not only probiotic powerhouses but also rich in essential nutrients like calcium, B vitamins, and protein. Kefir, in particular, is a great source of vitamin K2, which is important for bone and heart health.

5. Hydration and Refreshment:

- Lassi and ayran are traditionally consumed as refreshing beverages in hot climates, providing hydration while delivering probiotics and nutrients. These drinks can also help cool the body and replenish electrolytes.

Recipes
Homemade Kefir: Traditional and Flavored
Traditional Kefir
Ingredients:

- 1 quart (1 liter) whole milk (or any milk of your choice)
- 1-2 tablespoons kefir grains

Instructions:

1. Prepare the Milk: Pour the milk into a clean glass jar. If you're using raw milk, you can pasteurize it first by heating it to 145°F (63°C) for 30 minutes, then cooling it to room temperature.
2. Add Kefir Grains: Add the kefir grains to the milk, ensuring

they are fully submerged.

3. Ferment: Cover the jar with a clean cloth or coffee filter and secure it with a rubber band. Leave the jar at room temperature (68-77°F or 20-25°C) for 24-48 hours. The longer the fermentation, the tangier the kefir will be.

4. Strain and Store: Once the kefir has thickened and has a slightly tangy aroma, strain the grains using a plastic or non-metal strainer. Transfer the kefir to a clean jar and refrigerate it. The grains can be reused for the next batch.

5. Enjoy: Enjoy your kefir as is, or use it in smoothies, dressings, or as a base for flavored kefir.

Flavored Kefir
Ingredients:

- 1 quart (1 liter) traditional kefir
- 1 cup fresh or frozen fruits (e.g., berries, mango, peaches)
- 1-2 tablespoons honey or maple syrup (optional)
- 1 teaspoon vanilla extract (optional)

Instructions:

1. Blend: In a blender, combine the kefir, fruits, sweetener, and vanilla extract. Blend until smooth.

2. Chill and Serve: Pour the flavored kefir into a glass and serve chilled. Store any leftovers in the refrigerator for up to 3 days.

3. Lassi: Sweet and Savory Variations

Sweet Mango Lassi
Ingredients:

- 1 cup plain yogurt
- 1 ripe mango, peeled and diced
- 1/2 cup milk or water

- 2 tablespoons honey or sugar
- 1/4 teaspoon ground cardamom
- Ice cubes (optional)

Instructions:

1. Blend: In a blender, combine the yogurt, mango, milk or water, honey or sugar, and cardamom. Blend until smooth.
2. Serve: Pour into glasses, add ice cubes if desired, and serve chilled.

Savory Spiced Lassi
Ingredients:

- 1 cup plain yogurt
- 1/2 cup cold water
- 1/2 teaspoon roasted cumin powder
- 1/4 teaspoon black salt (kala namak)
- 1/4 teaspoon ground black pepper
- A pinch of chili powder or cayenne (optional)
- Fresh cilantro or mint leaves for garnish

Instructions:

1. Mix: In a bowl, whisk the yogurt and water until smooth. Add the cumin powder, black salt, black pepper, and chili powder, and stir well.
2. Serve: Pour into glasses, garnish with fresh cilantro or mint leaves, and serve chilled.

Ayran: A Refreshing Yogurt Drink
Ingredients:

- 1 cup plain yogurt
- 1/2 cup cold water
- A pinch of salt
- Ice cubes (optional)
- Fresh mint or dill for garnish (optional)

Instructions:

1. Blend: In a blender, combine the yogurt, water, and salt. Blend until smooth and frothy.
2. Serve: Pour into glasses, add ice cubes if desired, and garnish with fresh mint or dill. Serve immediately.

These recipes provide a delicious introduction to the world of fermented milk beverages. Whether you're enjoying a glass of traditional kefir, a sweet lassi, or a refreshing ayran, these drinks offer a unique combination of flavor, nutrition, and health benefits. Experiment with different flavors and ingredients to find your favorite versions of these timeless beverages.

Chapter 12: Whey Wonders: Using Every Drop

The Benefits of Whey and How to Use It

Whey is often considered a byproduct of cheese-making, but this versatile liquid is packed with nutrients and can be used in a variety of recipes. Rich in protein, vitamins, and minerals, whey has been a staple in many traditional diets around the world. This chapter explores the benefits of whey and offers recipes that maximize its potential, ensuring that every drop is put to good use.

The Benefits of Whey

1. High-Quality Protein Source:

- Whey is an excellent source of complete protein, containing all nine essential amino acids. This makes it particularly valuable for those looking to increase their protein intake, whether for muscle building, weight management, or overall health.

2. Rich in Vitamins and Minerals:

- Whey is not just about protein; it also contains significant amounts of calcium, B vitamins, and potassium. These nutrients contribute to bone health, energy production, and electrolyte balance.

3. Digestive Health:

- Whey contains lactose, a natural sugar that can be beneficial for gut health, particularly in fermented forms like whey kefir. It also has prebiotic properties, which can help support a healthy gut microbiome.

4. Hydration and Recovery:

- The electrolytes in whey make it a great option for rehydration and recovery after exercise. It helps replenish lost fluids and provides the body with the nutrients needed to repair and rebuild.

5. Sustainability and Zero Waste:

- Using whey in cooking and baking is a sustainable practice that reduces food waste. Instead of discarding this nutrient-rich liquid, it can be incorporated into various recipes, adding both flavor and nutrition.

Recipes
Whey Protein Smoothies
Ingredients:

- 1 cup whey (from yogurt or cheese-making)
- 1 banana, frozen or fresh
- 1/2 cup mixed berries (strawberries, blueberries, raspberries)
- 1 tablespoon honey or maple syrup (optional)
- 1 tablespoon chia seeds or flaxseeds (optional)
- 1/4 teaspoon vanilla extract (optional)
- Ice cubes (optional)

Instructions:

1. Blend: In a blender, combine the whey, banana, mixed berries, honey or maple syrup, chia seeds or flaxseeds, and vanilla extract. Blend until smooth.
2. Serve: Pour into a glass, add ice cubes if desired, and enjoy a refreshing, protein-packed smoothie.

Variations:

- Add a scoop of protein powder for an extra protein boost.
- Use different fruits like mango, peach, or pineapple for variety.
- Add a handful of spinach or kale for a green smoothie version.

Whey Bread
Ingredients:

- 3 cups all-purpose flour
- 1 cup whole wheat flour
- 1 1/2 cups warm whey (about 100°F or 38°C)
- 2 tablespoons honey
- 1 packet (2 1/4 teaspoons) active dry yeast
- 1 teaspoon salt
- 2 tablespoons olive oil or melted butter

Instructions:

1. Activate Yeast: In a large mixing bowl, combine the warm whey, honey, and yeast. Stir gently and let sit for 5-10 minutes until the mixture becomes frothy.
2. Mix Dough: Add the all-purpose flour, whole wheat flour, salt, and olive oil or melted butter to the yeast mixture. Stir until a dough forms.
3. Knead: Turn the dough onto a lightly floured surface and knead for about 8-10 minutes, until the dough is smooth and elastic.
4. First Rise: Place the dough in a greased bowl, cover with a clean cloth, and let it rise in a warm place for 1-2 hours, or until doubled in size.
5. Shape and Second Rise: Punch down the dough and shape it into a loaf. Place it in a greased loaf pan, cover, and let it rise

      again for 30-45 minutes.

6. Bake: Preheat the oven to 375°F (190°C). Bake the bread for 30-35 minutes, or until golden brown and the loaf sounds hollow when tapped on the bottom.

7. Cool: Let the bread cool in the pan for 10 minutes, then transfer it to a wire rack to cool completely before slicing.

Variations:

- Add seeds or nuts to the dough for added texture and flavor.
- Use whole wheat flour entirely for a denser, more nutritious loaf.
- Incorporate herbs like rosemary or thyme for a savory twist.

Whey-Based Soups and Sauces
Creamy Potato Soup with Whey
Ingredients:

- 4 large potatoes, peeled and diced
- 1 onion, chopped
- 2 cloves garlic, minced
- 4 cups whey
- 1 cup milk or cream
- 2 tablespoons butter
- Salt and pepper to taste
- Fresh chives or parsley for garnish

Instructions:

1. Sauté: In a large pot, melt the butter over medium heat. Add the chopped onion and garlic, and sauté until softened and fragrant.

2. Cook Potatoes: Add the diced potatoes to the pot, followed by the whey. Bring to a boil, then reduce heat and simmer for

15-20 minutes, or until the potatoes are tender.

3. Blend: Use an immersion blender to blend the soup until smooth. Alternatively, transfer the soup in batches to a blender and blend until smooth.

4. Add Cream: Stir in the milk or cream, and season with salt and pepper to taste.

5. Serve: Ladle the soup into bowls and garnish with fresh chives or parsley. Serve hot with crusty bread.

Variations:

- Add grated cheese for a richer, more indulgent soup.
- Incorporate other vegetables like carrots, celery, or leeks for added flavor and nutrition.
- Use whey as a base for other creamy soups, such as broccoli cheddar or cauliflower soup.

Whey Alfredo Sauce
Ingredients:

- 1 cup whey
- 1/2 cup heavy cream
- 1/2 cup grated Parmesan cheese
- 2 cloves garlic, minced
- 2 tablespoons butter
- Salt and pepper to taste
- Fresh parsley for garnish

Instructions:

1. Sauté Garlic: In a saucepan, melt the butter over medium heat. Add the minced garlic and sauté until fragrant.

2. Add Whey and Cream: Pour in the whey and heavy cream, stirring constantly. Bring the mixture to a simmer.

3. Add Cheese: Gradually stir in the grated Parmesan cheese, allowing it to melt and thicken the sauce.
4. Season: Season with salt and pepper to taste.
5. Serve: Toss the sauce with cooked pasta, and garnish with fresh parsley. Serve immediately.

Variations:

- Add cooked chicken, shrimp, or sautéed mushrooms for a heartier dish.
- Use the sauce as a base for a creamy lasagna or as a topping for steamed vegetables.
- Replace Parmesan with other cheeses like Pecorino Romano or Asiago for a different flavor profile.

Whey is a nutritional powerhouse that should never go to waste. By incorporating it into smoothies, bread, soups, and sauces, you can elevate your cooking and baking while reaping the health benefits of this often-overlooked ingredient. Whether you're looking to add protein to your diet, improve digestion, or simply explore new culinary possibilities, these recipes will help you make the most of every drop of whey.

Chapter 13: Ice Cream and Frozen Treats

Exploring the World of Frozen Milk-Based Desserts

Frozen milk-based desserts have long been cherished as delightful treats across cultures and climates. Whether it's the smooth, dense texture of gelato, the creamy richness of ice cream, or the refreshing lightness of sorbet and sherbet, these desserts offer a cooling escape and a sweet indulgence. This chapter delves into the fascinating world of frozen desserts, exploring the differences between gelato and ice cream, and offering recipes for various frozen delights.

Gelato vs. Ice Cream: Key Differences and Recipes

Gelato and ice cream are both beloved frozen desserts, but they differ in texture, flavor, and composition.

1. Texture and Ingredients:

- Gelato is known for its dense, silky texture. It contains less air than ice cream, giving it a richer mouthfeel. Gelato also has a higher proportion of milk to cream, resulting in a lower fat content compared to ice cream.
- Ice Cream is typically lighter and creamier due to a higher fat content and the incorporation of more air during the churning process. It often contains more cream than milk, contributing to its rich, creamy texture.

2. Temperature:

- Gelato is served at a slightly warmer temperature than ice cream, which enhances its flavor and gives it a softer consistency.
- Ice Cream is served at a colder temperature, which helps it maintain its firm, scoopable texture.

3. Flavor Profile:

- Gelato is known for its intense flavors, as the lower fat content allows the ingredients to shine through more vividly.
- Ice Cream offers a creamy, rich flavor, with a wide variety of options from classic vanilla and chocolate to more adventurous combinations.

Gelato Recipe
Ingredients:

- 2 cups whole milk
- 1 cup heavy cream
- 3/4 cup granulated sugar
- 4 large egg yolks
- 1 teaspoon vanilla extract (or flavor of your choice)

Instructions:

1. Heat Milk and Cream: In a saucepan, combine the milk and cream. Heat over medium heat until the mixture is warm, but not boiling.
2. Whisk Egg Yolks: In a separate bowl, whisk together the egg yolks and sugar until the mixture is pale and thick.
3. Temper the Eggs: Slowly pour the warm milk and cream mixture into the egg yolks, whisking constantly to prevent curdling.
4. Cook the Mixture: Return the mixture to the saucepan and cook over low heat, stirring constantly, until it thickens and coats the back of a spoon.
5. Cool and Churn: Remove from heat and stir in the vanilla extract. Let the mixture cool completely, then refrigerate for at least 4 hours. Once chilled, churn in an ice cream maker according to the manufacturer's instructions.
6. Freeze: Transfer the gelato to an airtight container and freeze

for at least 2 hours before serving.

Flavor Variations:

- Add 1/2 cup of pureed fruit, such as strawberries or mango, for a fruity gelato.
- Mix in finely chopped chocolate or nuts for added texture.
- Infuse the milk with coffee beans or tea leaves for a caffeinated twist.

Classic Ice Cream Recipe
Ingredients:

- 2 cups heavy cream
- 1 cup whole milk
- 3/4 cup granulated sugar
- 1 tablespoon vanilla extract (or flavor of your choice)
- Pinch of salt

Instructions:

1. Mix Ingredients: In a large mixing bowl, combine the heavy cream, milk, sugar, vanilla extract, and salt. Whisk until the sugar is dissolved.
2. Churn: Pour the mixture into an ice cream maker and churn according to the manufacturer's instructions until it reaches a soft-serve consistency.
3. Freeze: Transfer the ice cream to an airtight container and freeze for at least 4 hours or until firm.

Flavor Variations:

- Add 1/2 cup of crushed cookies, candy pieces, or chocolate chips during the last few minutes of churning.

- Swirl in caramel, fudge, or fruit preserves before freezing.
- Experiment with different extracts, like almond or peppermint, for unique flavors.

Sorbet and Sherbet

Sorbet and sherbet are lighter, fruit-based frozen desserts that provide a refreshing alternative to creamier options.

1. Sorbet:

- Sorbet is a dairy-free frozen dessert made primarily from fruit juice or puree, water, and sugar. It's light, refreshing, and intensely flavorful, making it a perfect palate cleanser or a cooling treat on a hot day.

2. Sherbet:

- Sherbet, on the other hand, is a hybrid between sorbet and ice cream. It contains a small amount of dairy (usually milk or cream), giving it a slightly creamier texture than sorbet but lighter than ice cream.

Lemon Sorbet Recipe
Ingredients:

- 1 cup freshly squeezed lemon juice (about 4-5 lemons)
- 1 cup water
- 3/4 cup granulated sugar
- Zest of 1 lemon
- 1 tablespoon lemon zest
- Pinch of salt

Instructions:

- Make Syrup: In a saucepan, combine the water, sugar, and

lemon zest. Heat over medium heat, stirring until the sugar is dissolved. Remove from heat and let it cool.

- Mix: Once cooled, stir in the lemon juice and a pinch of salt.
- Churn: Pour the mixture into an ice cream maker and churn according to the manufacturer's instructions.
- Freeze: Transfer the sorbet to an airtight container and freeze for at least 2 hours before serving.

Variations:

- Substitute lemon juice with lime, grapefruit, or orange juice for different citrus flavors.
- Add a splash of vodka or limoncello for an adult twist.

Orange Sherbet Recipe
Ingredients:

- 2 cups freshly squeezed orange juice (about 5-6 oranges)
- 1/2 cup whole milk
- 1/2 cup heavy cream
- 3/4 cup granulated sugar
- 1 tablespoon orange zest

Instructions:

1. Mix Ingredients: In a mixing bowl, whisk together the orange juice, milk, cream, sugar, and orange zest until the sugar is dissolved.
2. Churn: Pour the mixture into an ice cream maker and churn according to the manufacturer's instructions.
3. Freeze: Transfer the sherbet to an airtight container and freeze for at least 4 hours or until firm.

Variations:

- Mix in finely chopped mint or basil for a refreshing herbal flavor.
- Add a splash of Grand Marnier or Cointreau for an orange liqueur-infused sherbet.

Milk-Based Frozen Yogurt

Frozen yogurt offers a tangy, creamy alternative to ice cream, with the added benefits of probiotics from live cultures.

Vanilla Frozen Yogurt Recipe

Ingredients:

- 2 cups plain Greek yogurt
- 1/2 cup heavy cream
- 1/2 cup granulated sugar
- 1 teaspoon vanilla extract

Instructions:

- Mix Ingredients: In a mixing bowl, whisk together the Greek yogurt, heavy cream, sugar, and vanilla extract until smooth.
- Churn: Pour the mixture into an ice cream maker and churn according to the manufacturer's instructions.
- Freeze: Transfer the frozen yogurt to an airtight container and freeze for at least 2 hours before serving.

Flavor Variations:

- Add fresh or frozen berries, chopped nuts, or chocolate chips for added texture.
- Swirl in honey or fruit preserves for extra sweetness.
- Experiment with different extracts, such as almond, lemon, or coconut, for unique flavors.

Frozen milk-based desserts are more than just a treat—they are an art form that balances creaminess, sweetness, and flavor. Whether you prefer the rich indulgence of ice cream, the intense flavors of gelato, the refreshing lightness of sorbet, or the tangy delight of frozen yogurt, this chapter provides the knowledge and recipes to create these delicious desserts at home.

Chapter 14: Condiments and Dressings

Creating Rich, Milk-Based Condiments

Condiments and dressings play a crucial role in enhancing the flavors of various dishes. Milk-based dressings and sauces add a creamy, rich texture that elevates salads, sandwiches, and grilled meats. In this chapter, we'll explore how to create classic, flavorful condiments using milk derivatives such as buttermilk, yogurt, and cream.

Ranch Dressing

Ranch dressing is a creamy, tangy dressing made with buttermilk, mayonnaise, and a blend of herbs and spices. It's a versatile condiment that pairs well with salads, vegetables, and even as a dipping sauce for chicken wings or fries.

Ingredients:

- 1/2 cup buttermilk
- 1/2 cup mayonnaise
- 1/4 cup sour cream
- 1 tablespoon chopped fresh parsley
- 1 tablespoon chopped fresh dill
- 1 tablespoon chopped fresh chives
- 1 garlic clove, minced
- 1 teaspoon onion powder
- 1 teaspoon lemon juice
- Salt and pepper to taste

Instructions:

1. Mix the Base: In a medium bowl, whisk together the buttermilk, mayonnaise, and sour cream until smooth.
2. Add Herbs and Spices: Stir in the parsley, dill, chives, garlic,

onion powder, and lemon juice. Mix well to combine.

3. Season: Season with salt and pepper to taste. Adjust the seasoning as needed.

4. Chill and Serve: Cover and refrigerate the dressing for at least 30 minutes to allow the flavors to meld. Serve cold with salads, as a dip, or as a spread on sandwiches.

Variations:

- Add a pinch of cayenne pepper or hot sauce for a spicy kick.
- Substitute the mayonnaise with Greek yogurt for a lighter version.
- Experiment with different herbs like basil or cilantro for a unique flavor twist.

Blue Cheese Dressing

Blue cheese dressing is a rich, tangy dressing made with crumbled blue cheese, mayonnaise, and sour cream. It's perfect for drizzling over salads, especially wedge salads, or as a dipping sauce for buffalo wings.

Ingredients:

- 1/2 cup crumbled blue cheese
- 1/4 cup buttermilk
- 1/4 cup mayonnaise
- 1/4 cup sour cream
- 1 tablespoon white wine vinegar
- 1 teaspoon lemon juice
- 1/2 teaspoon garlic powder
- Salt and pepper to taste

Instructions:

1. Combine the Base: In a medium bowl, whisk together the mayonnaise, sour cream, buttermilk, vinegar, lemon juice, and

garlic powder until smooth.

2. Add the Blue Cheese: Gently fold in the crumbled blue cheese. Mix well, leaving some chunks for texture.

3. Season: Season with salt and pepper to taste. Adjust the thickness by adding more buttermilk if a thinner consistency is desired.

4. Chill and Serve: Cover and refrigerate for at least 1 hour before serving to allow the flavors to develop. Serve with salads, as a dip, or as a sauce for steak or burgers.

Variations:

- Add a tablespoon of chopped fresh parsley or chives for added freshness.
- For a more intense blue cheese flavor, increase the amount of crumbled blue cheese.
- Use Greek yogurt instead of sour cream for a tangier version.

Tzatziki Sauce

Tzatziki is a creamy Greek sauce made from yogurt, cucumber, garlic, and dill. It's a refreshing condiment that pairs well with grilled meats, vegetables, and pita bread.

Ingredients:

- 1 cup plain Greek yogurt
- 1/2 cucumber, grated and drained
- 2 garlic cloves, minced
- 1 tablespoon olive oil
- 1 tablespoon lemon juice
- 1 tablespoon chopped fresh dill
- Salt and pepper to taste

Instructions:

1. Prepare the Cucumber: Grate the cucumber using a box grater. Place the grated cucumber in a clean kitchen towel or cheesecloth and squeeze out the excess liquid.
2. Mix the Base: In a medium bowl, combine the Greek yogurt, minced garlic, olive oil, lemon juice, and dill.
3. Add the Cucumber: Stir in the grated cucumber until well combined.
4. Season: Season with salt and pepper to taste. Adjust the lemon juice and dill to your preference.
5. Chill and Serve: Cover and refrigerate the tzatziki for at least 30 minutes to allow the flavors to meld. Serve cold with grilled meats, vegetables, or as a dip with pita bread.

Variations:

- Add a pinch of cayenne pepper or hot sauce for a spicy twist.
- Substitute dill with mint for a different flavor profile.
- Use regular plain yogurt instead of Greek yogurt for a thinner consistency.

Milk-based condiments like Ranch Dressing, Blue Cheese Dressing, and Tzatziki Sauce add a rich, creamy element to various dishes. By mastering these recipes, you can enhance the flavor of your meals and create delicious, homemade alternatives to store-bought dressings.

Chapter 15: Baking with Milk Derivatives

Incorporating Milk Derivatives into Baked Goods

Milk derivatives like buttermilk, cream cheese, and milk are essential ingredients in baking. They add moisture, richness, and tang to a variety of baked goods, enhancing flavor and texture. This chapter explores how to use these ingredients to create classic, delicious baked treats that showcase the versatility of milk derivatives.

Buttermilk Pancakes

Buttermilk pancakes are a breakfast favorite, known for their fluffy texture and slightly tangy flavor. The acidity of the buttermilk reacts with baking soda, creating a light and airy pancake that's perfect for soaking up syrup or topped with fresh fruit.

Ingredients:

- 2 cups all-purpose flour
- 2 tablespoons granulated sugar
- 2 teaspoons baking powder
- 1 teaspoon baking soda
- 1/2 teaspoon salt
- 2 cups buttermilk
- 2 large eggs
- 1/4 cup unsalted butter, melted
- 1 teaspoon vanilla extract

Instructions:

1. Prepare the Dry Ingredients: In a large mixing bowl, whisk together the flour, sugar, baking powder, baking soda, and salt.
2. Mix the Wet Ingredients: In a separate bowl, whisk together the buttermilk, eggs, melted butter, and vanilla extract.

3. Combine: Pour the wet ingredients into the dry ingredients and stir until just combined. The batter should be lumpy—avoid overmixing to prevent tough pancakes.

4. Cook the Pancakes: Heat a griddle or large skillet over medium heat and lightly grease it with butter or oil. Pour 1/4 cup of batter onto the griddle for each pancake. Cook until bubbles form on the surface, then flip and cook until golden brown on the other side.

5. Serve: Serve the pancakes warm with butter, syrup, or your favorite toppings.

Variations:

- Add 1/2 cup of fresh berries, chocolate chips, or nuts to the batter for added flavor and texture.
- Substitute part of the all-purpose flour with whole wheat flour for a heartier pancake.
- For a citrusy twist, add a tablespoon of lemon or orange zest to the batter.

Cream Cheese Frosting

Cream cheese frosting is a rich, tangy topping that pairs perfectly with cakes, cupcakes, and cinnamon rolls. Its creamy texture and slight tartness balance the sweetness of desserts, making it a versatile frosting option.

Ingredients:

- 8 oz cream cheese, softened
- 1/2 cup unsalted butter, softened
- 4 cups powdered sugar
- 1 teaspoon vanilla extract

- Pinch of salt

Instructions:

1. Beat the Cream Cheese and Butter: In a large mixing bowl, beat the softened cream cheese and butter together using an electric mixer until smooth and creamy, about 2-3 minutes.
2. Add the Sugar: Gradually add the powdered sugar, one cup at a time, beating on low speed until incorporated. Once all the sugar is added, increase the speed to medium-high and beat until light and fluffy.
3. Flavor and Season: Add the vanilla extract and a pinch of salt. Beat until well combined.
4. Use: Spread the frosting on cakes, cupcakes, or any baked goods that need a rich, creamy topping.

Variations:

- For a citrus-flavored frosting, add a tablespoon of lemon or orange zest.
- Mix in 1/4 cup of cocoa powder for a chocolate cream cheese frosting.
- Add a tablespoon of heavy cream for a slightly lighter, more spreadable consistency.

Milk Bread

Milk bread, also known as Hokkaido milk bread, is a soft, fluffy loaf with a tender crumb and slightly sweet flavor. The addition of milk gives the bread its characteristic texture, making it perfect for sandwiches, toast, or simply enjoying with butter.

Ingredients:

- 3 1/4 cups bread flour
- 3 tablespoons granulated sugar
- 2 teaspoons active dry yeast
- 1 teaspoon salt
- 1/2 cup whole milk, warm
- 1/4 cup heavy cream, warm
- 1/4 cup water, warm
- 1 large egg
- 4 tablespoons unsalted butter, softened

Instructions:

1. Activate the Yeast: In a small bowl, combine the warm milk, heavy cream, water, and sugar. Sprinkle the yeast over the mixture and let it sit for 5-10 minutes until foamy.
2. Mix the Dough: In a large mixing bowl, combine the flour and salt. Add the yeast mixture and the egg. Mix until a sticky dough forms.
3. Knead the Dough: Add the softened butter to the dough and knead until the butter is fully incorporated and the dough is smooth and elastic, about 10 minutes by hand or 5 minutes with a stand mixer.
4. First Rise: Place the dough in a greased bowl, cover it with a clean kitchen towel, and let it rise in a warm place until it doubles in size, about 1 to 1 1/2 hours.
5. Shape the Dough: Punch down the dough to release the air. Divide it into four equal pieces and shape each piece into a ball. Place the dough balls into a greased loaf pan, side by side.
6. Second Rise: Cover the pan with a towel and let the dough rise again until it has doubled in size, about 45 minutes.
7. Bake: Preheat the oven to 350°F (175°C). Brush the top of the dough with a little milk or egg wash for a shiny finish. Bake for 25-30 minutes, or until the bread is golden brown and sounds

hollow when tapped.

8. Cool: Let the bread cool in the pan for 10 minutes before transferring it to a wire rack to cool completely.

Variations:

- Add 1/4 cup of sugar to the dough for a sweeter loaf, perfect for French toast.
- Incorporate 1/2 cup of raisins or dried fruit for a fruit-studded milk bread.
- Use a tangzhong (water roux) method for an even softer, fluffier loaf.

Incorporating milk derivatives like buttermilk, cream cheese, and milk into your baking can transform ordinary recipes into extraordinary ones. Whether you're making light and fluffy pancakes, a rich and tangy frosting, or a soft and pillowy loaf of bread, these recipes showcase the delicious potential of dairy in the world of baking.

Conclusion: Embracing the Art of Dairy
The Satisfaction of Homemade Dairy

In a world where convenience often takes precedence, there is something uniquely rewarding about crafting your own dairy products at home. The process of transforming simple cow's milk into an array of delicious derivatives—whether it's a batch of creamy yogurt, a loaf of tender milk bread, or a wedge of aged cheddar—connects us to traditional practices that have been passed down through generations. The sights, sounds, and smells of dairy processing evoke a sense of nostalgia and accomplishment that is hard to find in store-bought products.

Homemade dairy allows you to control the quality of your ingredients, ensuring that you are consuming wholesome, fresh products without unnecessary additives or preservatives. The flavors are richer, the textures more satisfying, and the experience of creating something from scratch is deeply fulfilling. Whether you're making your own butter for the first time or perfecting your cheese-aging technique, each step in the process is a reminder of the beauty and versatility of dairy.

Encouragement to Experiment with Milk Derivatives in Cooking

As you've explored throughout this book, cow's milk is one of the most versatile ingredients in the kitchen. From the basics of fresh cream and butter to the complexities of cheese and yogurt, the potential for culinary creativity is nearly limitless. I encourage you to take what you've learned and experiment further. Try your hand at new recipes, explore different cultures' uses of dairy, and don't be afraid to push the boundaries of traditional techniques.

Consider making variations on the recipes provided, or inventing your own unique dishes that highlight the flavors and textures of milk derivatives. Experiment with infusing different herbs and spices into your dairy products, or explore the world of non-dairy alternatives to create vegan versions of your favorite dishes. The possibilities are endless, and each new discovery will deepen your appreciation for the art of dairy.

In embracing the art of dairy, you are not just learning to cook—you are becoming a part of a long-standing culinary tradition. With each recipe, you are preserving the knowledge and skills that have sustained communities for centuries, while also contributing your own modern twist to this timeless craft. So, gather your ingredients, trust the process, and enjoy the journey. The world of dairy is vast and varied, and it's yours to explore.